Music Group Choruses

Book Three

Arranged for C, B flat, E flat and Bass Clef
instruments, keyboard and guitar by

Keith Stent

Kevin Mayhew

We hope you enjoy *Music Group Choruses* Book 3.
Further copies of this and the other books in the series
are available from your local music shop.

In case of difficulty, please contact the publisher direct:

The Sales Department
KEVIN MAYHEW LTD
Rattlesden
Bury St Edmunds
Suffolk IP30 0SZ

Phone 01449 737978
Fax 01449 737834

Please ask for our complete catalogue of outstanding Church Music.

Acknowledgement

We wish to express our gratitude to the copyright holders for
permission to use copyright material in this publication.
Full details are given beneath each individual piece.

Front Cover: *The Music Party*
by Franz Xavier Hendrick Verbeeck (1685-1755).
Courtesy of Johnny van Haeften Gallery, London/The Bridgeman Art Library,
London. Reproduced by kind permission.

Cover designed by Graham Johnstone and Veronica Ward.

First published in Great Britain in 1996 by Kevin Mayhew Ltd.

© Copyright 1996 Kevin Mayhew Ltd.

ISBN 0 86209 888 2
Catalogue No: 1400104

0 1 2 3 4 5 6 7 8 9

Music Editors: Rosalind Dean and Stephanie Hill
Music setting by Daniel Kelly

Printed and bound in Great Britain by
Caligraving Limited Thetford Norfolk

Contents

Arranger's Note

These arrangements are intended to be as flexible as possible. All of the instrumental parts may be played separately or combined; the C and B♭ instruments are provided with an alternative part which may be played as well as or instead of the first part.

KEITH STENT

1 AT YOUR FEET WE FALL

David Fellingham

2 BY YOUR SIDE

Noel and Tricia Richards

3 FATHER GOD I WONDER *I will sing your praises*

Ian Smale

Lyrics:
Fa - ther God I won - der how I man - aged to ex - ist with - out the
know-ledge of your par - ent - hood and your lov - ing care. But

now I am your son, I am a-dopt-ed in your fa-mi-ly and

Em   D

I can ne-ver be a-lone, 'cause Fa-ther God you're there be-side me.

C   D   B⁷

4 GLORY

glo - ry to the Lamb of God, and glo - ry to the liv - ing word;

G D Csus² G D Csus²

glo - ry to the Lamb!

G D C D Gsus²

5 I WILL ENTER HIS GATES

Leona von Brethorst

6 JESUS, JESUS *Holy and anointed one*

John Barnett

7 JESUS PUT THIS SONG INTO OUR HEARTS

Graham Kendrick

8 MAJESTY

Jack W. Hayford

Music Group Choruses

Book Three

1   AT YOUR FEET WE FALL

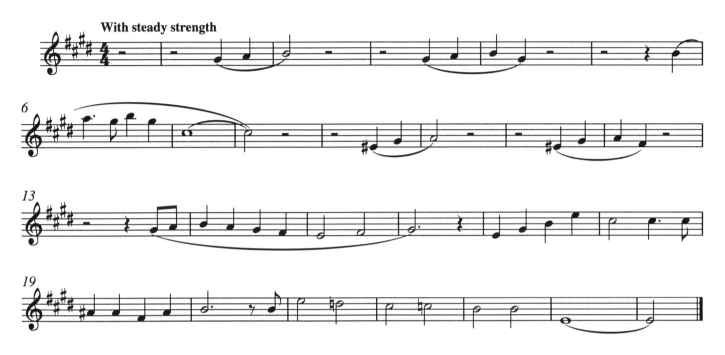

2   BY YOUR SIDE

3 FATHER GOD I WONDER *I will sing your praises*

4 GLORY

5 I WILL ENTER HIS GATES

6 JESUS, JESUS *Holy and anointed*

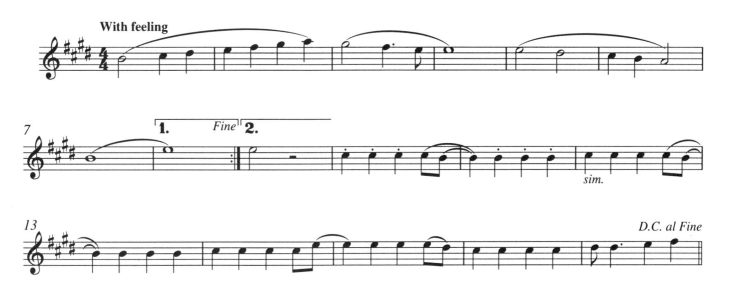

7 JESUS PUT THIS SONG INTO OUR HEARTS

'Hebrew' style, getting faster

8 MAJESTY

Triumphantly

9   OUR CONFIDENCE IS IN THE LORD

10 RESTORE, O LORD

11 SUCH LOVE

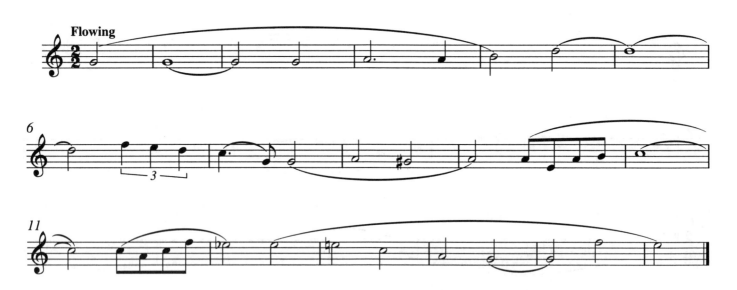

12 WE'LL WALK THE LAND *Let the flame burn brighter*

13 YOU ARE CROWNED WITH MANY CROWNS

Music Group Choruses

Book Three

1 AT YOUR FEET WE FALL

2 BY YOUR SIDE

3 FATHER GOD I WONDER *I will sing your praises*

4 GLORY

5   I WILL ENTER HIS GATES

6 JESUS, JESUS *Holy and anointed one*

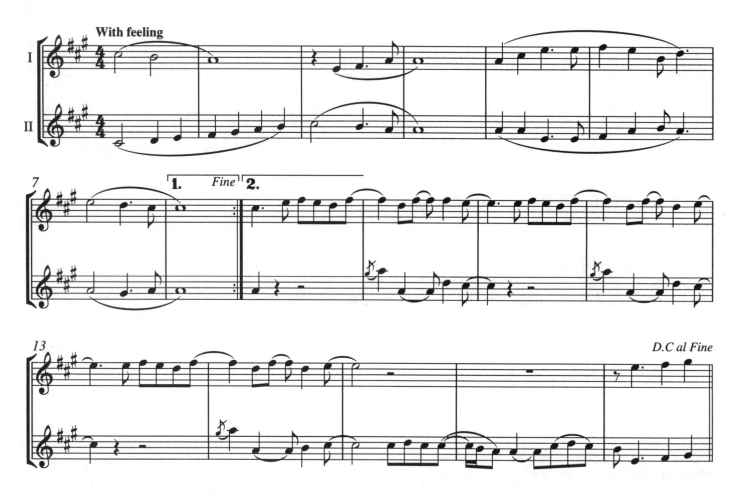

7 JESUS PUT THIS SONG INTO OUR HEARTS

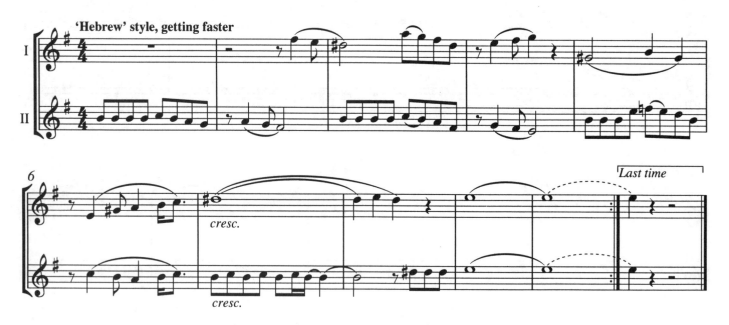

8 MAJESTY

9 OUR CONFIDENCE IS IN THE LORD

10 RESTORE, O LORD

11 SUCH LOVE

12 WE'LL WALK THE LAND *Let the flame burn brighter*

13 YOU ARE CROWNED WITH MANY CROWNS

Music Group Choruses

Book Three

1 AT YOUR FEET WE FALL

2 BY YOUR SIDE

3 FATHER GOD I WONDER *I will sing your praises*

4 GLORY

5 I WILL ENTER HIS GATES

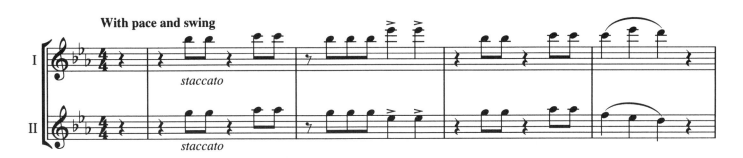

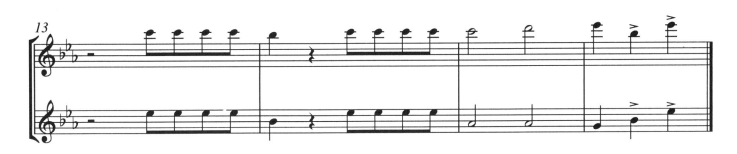

6 JESUS, JESUS *Holy and anointed one*

7 JESUS PUT THIS SONG INTO OUR HEARTS

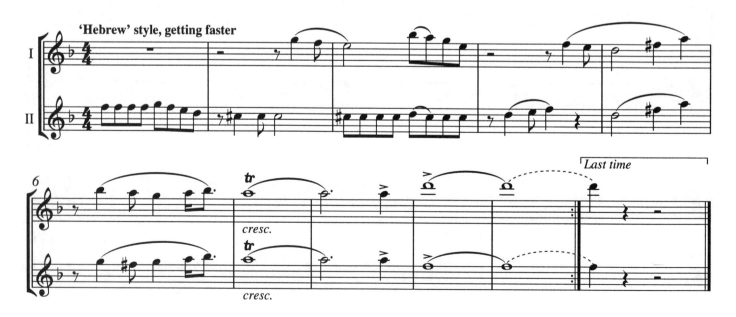

8 MAJESTY

9 OUR CONFIDENCE IS IN THE LORD

10 RESTORE, O LORD

11 SUCH LOVE

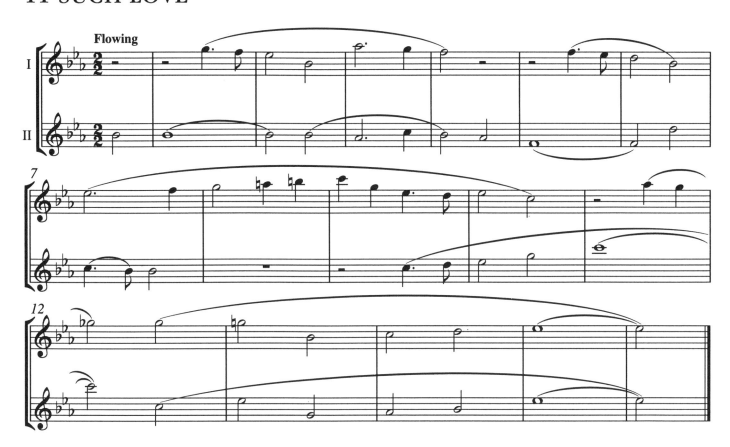

12 WE'LL WALK THE LAND *Let the flame burn brighter*

13 YOU ARE CROWNED WITH MANY CROWNS

Music Group Choruses

Book Three

1 AT YOUR FEET WE FALL

2 BY YOUR SIDE

3 FATHER GOD I WONDER *I will sing your praises*

4 GLORY

5 I WILL ENTER HIS GATES

6 JESUS, JESUS *Holy and anointed one*

7 JESUS PUT THIS SONG INTO OUR HEARTS

8 MAJESTY

9 OUR CONFIDENCE IS IN THE LORD

With strength

10 RESTORE, O LORD

Steadily, with feeling

11 SUCH LOVE

12 WE'LL WALK THE LAND *Let the flame burn brighter*

13 YOU ARE CROWNED WITH MANY CROWNS

With a strong rhythm

5

9

13

17

22

Ma - jes-ty,   wor-ship his ma - jes-ty,   Je - sus who

G   C   Am   D⁷

died;   now glo - ri - fied,   King of all kings.

G   Em⁷   Am   D   G   C   G

9 OUR CONFIDENCE IS IN THE LORD

Noel and Tricia Richards

He is our for-tress, we will ne-ver be sha - ken. He is our for-tress, we will ne-ver be sha - ken.

D   Em   D   G

We   will put our   trust   in   God.

G   A   Bm

We will put our trust in God.

Our God.

10 RESTORE, O LORD

Graham Kendrick and Chris Rolinson

Steadily, with feeling

men may see and come with rev – 'rent fear to the liv – ing God

Em⁷   A   D   F♯   Bm   Bm/A   Gmaj⁷   F♯m⁷   Em⁷

whose king – dom   shall out – last   the years.

G/A   Gmaj⁹   Em⁷   G   D

11 SUCH LOVE

Graham Kendrick

12 WE'LL WALK THE LAND *Let the flame burn brighter*

Graham Kendrick

1. We'll walk the land with hearts on fire; and ev-'ry step will be a prayer. Hope is ris - ing, new day dawn - ing; sound of sing - ing fills the

loud - er, as our love grows strong - er; let it shine! Let it

Gm
Em

Dm
Bm

C
A

Bb
G

Dm7
Bm7

C
A

shine!

3. We'll walk for

F
D

Bb
G

Dm7
Bm7

C
A

13 YOU ARE CROWNED WITH MANY CROWNS

John Sellers

With a strong rhythm

You are crowned with ma - ny crowns, and rule all things in right - eous - ness.

You are crowned with ma - ny crowns, up - hold - ing all things by your word.

Texts

1 AT YOUR FEET WE FALL

1 At your feet we fall, mighty risen Lord,
as we come before your throne to worship you.
By your Spirit's power you now draw our hearts,
and we hear your voice in triumph ringing clear.

Refrain
I am he that liveth, that liveth and was dead.
Behold, I am alive for evermore.

2 There we see you stand, mighty risen Lord,
clothed in garments pure and holy, shining bright.
Eyes of flashing fire, feet like burnished bronze,
and the sound of many waters is your voice.

3 Like the shining sun in its noonday strength,
we now see the glory of your wondrous face.
Once that face was marred, but now you're glorified,
and your words like a two-edged sword
have mighty power.

2 BY YOUR SIDE

1 By your side I would stay;
in your arms I would lay.
Jesus, lover of my soul,
nothing from you I withhold.
Lord, I love you, and adore you;
what more can I say?
You cause my love to grow stronger
with ev'ry passing day.

3 FATHER GOD I WONDER
(I will sing your praises)

Father God I wonder
how I managed to exist
without the knowledge of your parenthood
and your loving care.
But now I am your son,
I am adopted
in your family
and I can never be alone,
'cause Father God you're there beside me.
I will sing your praises, I will sing your praises,
I will sing your praises for evermore.

4 GLORY

Glory, glory in the highest;
glory, to the Almighty; glory to the Lamb of God,
and glory to the living word;
glory to the Lamb!

Refrain
I give glory, *glory*, glory, *glory*,
glory, glory to the Lamb!
I give glory, *glory*, glory, *glory*,
glory, glory to the Lamb!
I give glory to the Lamb!

5 I WILL ENTER HIS GATES

I will enter his gates with thanksgiving in my heart,
I will enter his courts with praise,
I will say this is the day that the Lord has made,
I will rejoice for he has made me glad.
He has made me glad, (2)
I will rejoice for he has made me glad.
He has made me glad, (2)
I will rejoice for he has made me glad.

6 JESUS, JESUS
(Holy and anointed one)

Jesus, Jesus, holy and anointed one, Jesus.
Jesus, Jesus, risen and exalted one, Jesus.
Your name is like honey on my lips,
your spirit like water to my soul,
your word is a lamp unto my feet,
Jesus, I love you, I love you.

7 JESUS PUT THIS SONG INTO OUR HEARTS

1 Jesus put this song into our hearts, (2)
it's a song of joy no one can take away,
Jesus put this song into our hearts.

2 Jesus taught us how to live in harmony, (2)
Different faces, different races, he made us one,
Jesus taught us how to live in harmony.

3 Jesus taught us how to be a family, (2)
Loving one another with the love that he gives,
Jesus taught us how to be a family.

4 Jesus turned our sorrow into dancing, (2)
Changed our tears of sadness into rivers of joy,
Jesus turned our sorrow into a dance.

5 *Instrumental.*

8   MAJESTY

Majesty, worship his majesty,
unto Jesus be glory, honour and praise.
Majesty, kingdom authority,
flows from his throne unto his own,
his anthem raise.
So exalt, lift up on high the name of Jesus;
magnify, come glorify Christ Jesus the King.
Majesty, worship his majesty,
Jesus who died, now glorified,
King of all kings.

9   OUR CONFIDENCE IS IN THE LORD

Our confidence is in the Lord,
the source of our salvation.
Rest is found in him alone, the author of creation.
We will not fear the evil day,
because we have a refuge;
in ev'ry circumstance we say,
our hope is built on Jesus.

Refrain
He is our fortress, we will never be shaken. (4)
We will put our trust in God. (2)

10   RESTORE, O LORD

1   Restore, O Lord, the honour of your name,
in works of sov'reign power
come, shake the earth again,
that men may see
and come with rev'rent fear
to the living God
whose kingdom shall outlast the years.

2   Restore, O Lord,
In all the earth your fame,
and in our time revive
the church that bears your name.
And in your anger,
Lord, remember mercy,
O living God,
whose mercy shall outlast the years.

3   Bend us, O Lord,
where we are hard and cold,
in your refiner's fire
come purify the gold.
Though suffering comes
and evil crouches near,
still our living God
is reigning, he is reigning here.

4.   *As verse 1*

11   SUCH LOVE

1   Such love, pure as the whitest snow;
such love, weeps for the shame I know;
such love, paying the debt I owe;
O Jesus, such love.

2   Such love, stilling my restlessness;
such love, filling my emptiness;
such love, showing me holiness;
O Jesus, such love.

3   Such love, springs from eternity;
such love, streaming through history;
such love, fountain of life to me;
O Jesus, such love.

12   WE'LL WALK THE LAND
(Let the flame burn brighter)

1   We'll walk the land with hearts on fire;
and ev'ry step will be a prayer.
Hope is rising, new day dawning;
sound of singing fills the air.

2   Two thousand years, and still the flame
is burning bright across the land.
Hearts are waiting, longing, aching,
for awakening once again.

Refrain
Let the flame burn brighter
in the heart of the darkness,
turning night to glorious day.
Let the song grow louder,
as our love grows stronger;
let it shine! Let it shine!

3   We'll walk for truth, speak out for love;
In Jesus' name we shall be strong,
to lift the fallen, to save the children,
to fill the nation with your song.

Refrain

13   YOU ARE CROWNED WITH MANY CROWNS

You are crowned with many crowns,
and rule all things in righteousness.
You are crowned with many crowns,
upholding all things by your word.
You rule in power and reign in glory!
You are Lord of heaven and earth!
You are Lord of all. (2)